Asteroids & Meteoroids

by Grace Hansen

Abdo
OUR GALAXY
Kids

abdopublishing.com

Published by Abdo Kids, a division of ABDO, P.O. Box 398166, Minneapolis, Minnesota 55439.

Printed in the United States of America, North Mankato, Minnesota.

052017

092017

 THIS BOOK CONTAINS
RECYCLED MATERIALS

Photo Credits: iStock, NASA, Science Source, Shutterstock, ©Samuel Hansen p.19 / CC-BY-SA 2.0

Production Contributors: Teddy Borth, Jennie Forsberg, Grace Hansen

Design Contributors: Dorothy Toth, Laura Mitchell

Publisher's Cataloging in Publication Data

Names: Hansen, Grace, author.

Title: Asteroids & meteoroids / by Grace Hansen.

Other titles: Asteroids and meteors

Description: Minneapolis, Minnesota : Abdo Kids, 2018 | Series: Our galaxy |
    Includes bibliographical references and index.

Identifiers: LCCN 2016962401 | ISBN 9781532100499 (lib. bdg.) |
    ISBN 9781532101182 (ebook) | ISBN 9781532101731 (Read-to-me ebook)

Subjects: LCSH: Asteroids--Juvenile literature. | Meteoroids--Juvenile literature.

Classification: DDC 523.44--dc23

LC record available at http://lccn.loc.gov/2016962401

Table of Contents

How Asteroids Formed

Around 4.6 billion years ago our **solar system** formed. **Gravity** combined dust and gas over millions of years. This is how the sun was created.

Asteroids

Dust and gas then **orbited** the sun. They collided and formed lumps of rock and metal. The lumps crashed into each other and broke into pieces. These pieces are what we call asteroids.

6

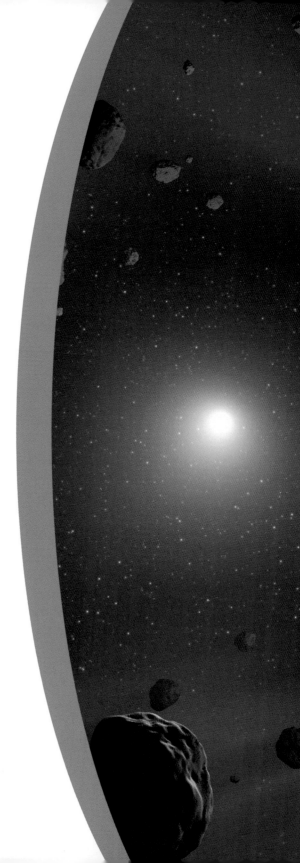

Most asteroids in our **solar system** are in the asteroid belt. This belt is between Mars and Jupiter.

Moon

Earth

Mars

asteroid belt

Jupiter

Some asteroid groups are outside of the asteroid belt. Most Trojan asteroids are found in Jupiter's **orbit**. Hilda asteroids form three major groups, making a triangle.

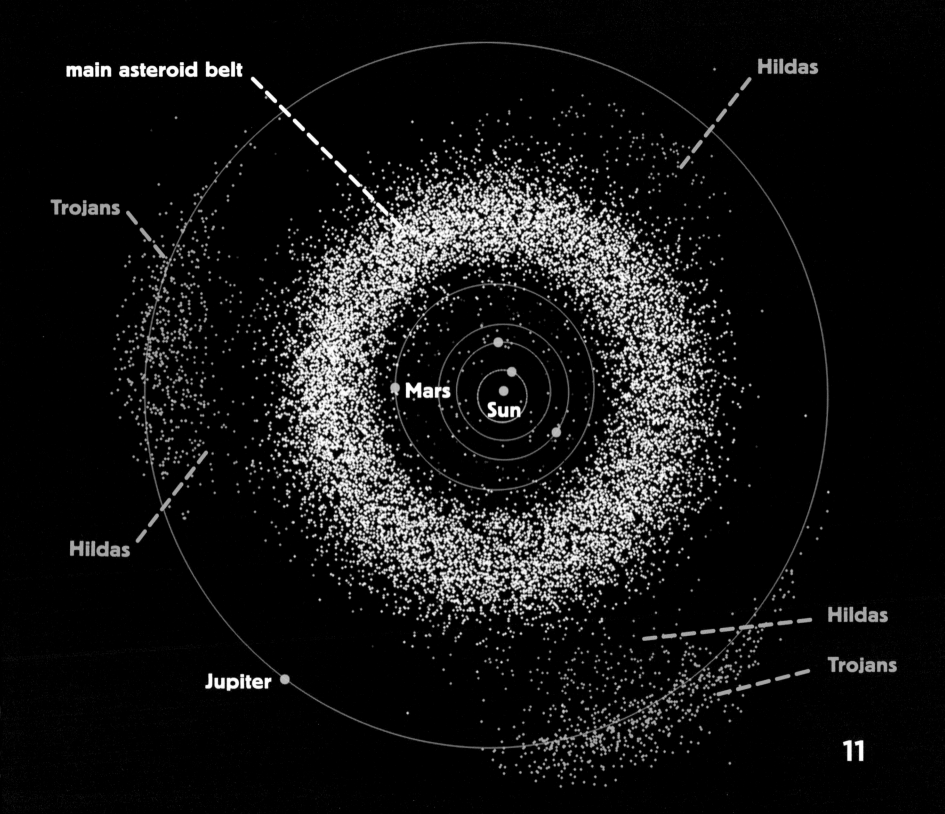

main asteroid belt

Hildas

Trojans

Hildas

Hildas

Trojans

Jupiter

Mars

Sun

11

Meteoroids

Meteoroids are also found in
the asteroid belt. They are
smaller pieces of asteroids.
They are often the size of a fist.

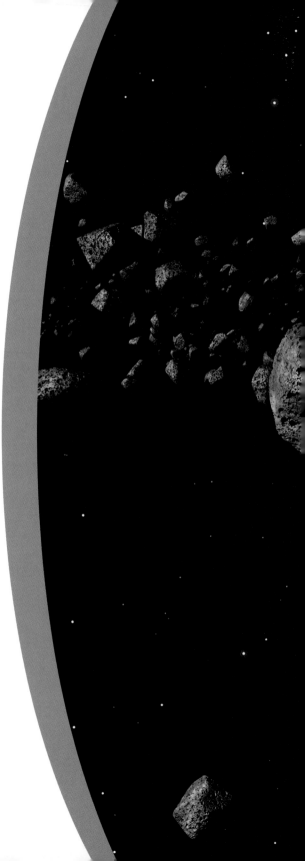

13

Meteors & Meteorites

Earth's **gravity** can pull in nearby meteoroids. The meteoroid passes through Earth's **atmosphere**.

14

The meteoroid moves fast. This causes **friction**. Friction makes heat. The heat makes light. This streak of light is called a meteor.

Most meteoroids burn
up. But some reach Earth.
These are called meteorites.

The Holsinger Meteorite is the largest discovered fragment of the 150-foot (45-meter) meteor that created Meteor Crater.

19

Large asteroids can also

hit Earth. These can cause

a lot of damage.

More Facts

- Many scientists agree that an asteroid hit Earth 65 million years ago. It may be what caused the dinosaurs to die out.

- There are billions of asteroids and meteoroids in our **solar system**.

- A long time ago, asteroids often hit Earth's moon. That is why the moon is full of craters.

Glossary

atmosphere – the whole mass of gases surrounding the earth.

friction – the resistance that one object encounters when moving over another.

gravity – the force by which all objects in the universe are attracted to each other.

orbit – the curved path of a planet, moon, or other object around a larger celestial body.

solar system – a group of planets and other celestial bodies that are held by the sun's gravity and revolve around it.

Index

abdokids.com

Use this code to log on to abdokids.com and access crafts, games, videos and more!

Abdo Kids Code:
OAK0499